TANGLE MANDALA
COLORING BOOK FOR ADULTS

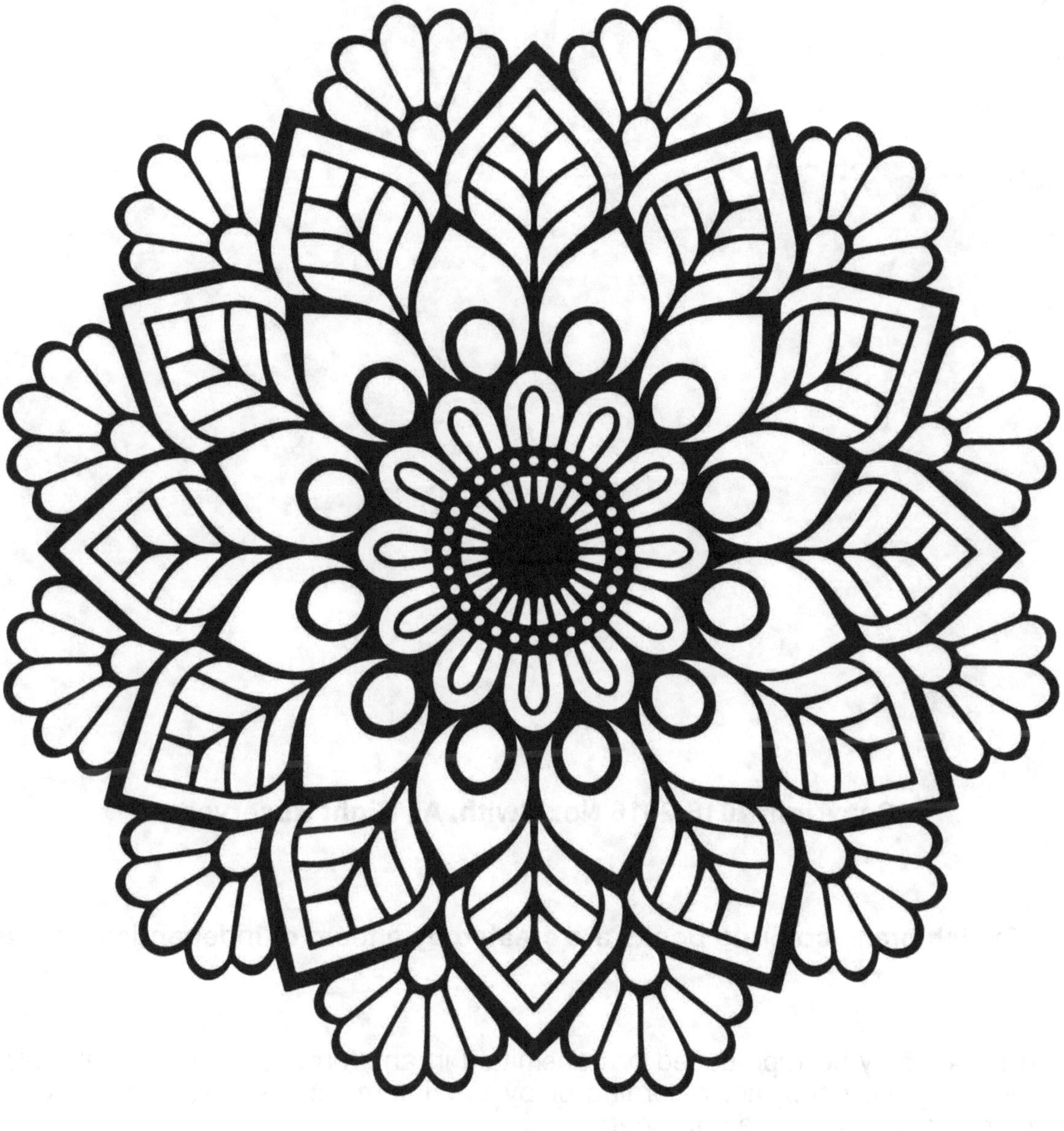

NOX SMITH

Nox Switch brand coloring books are created by a team of independent artists.

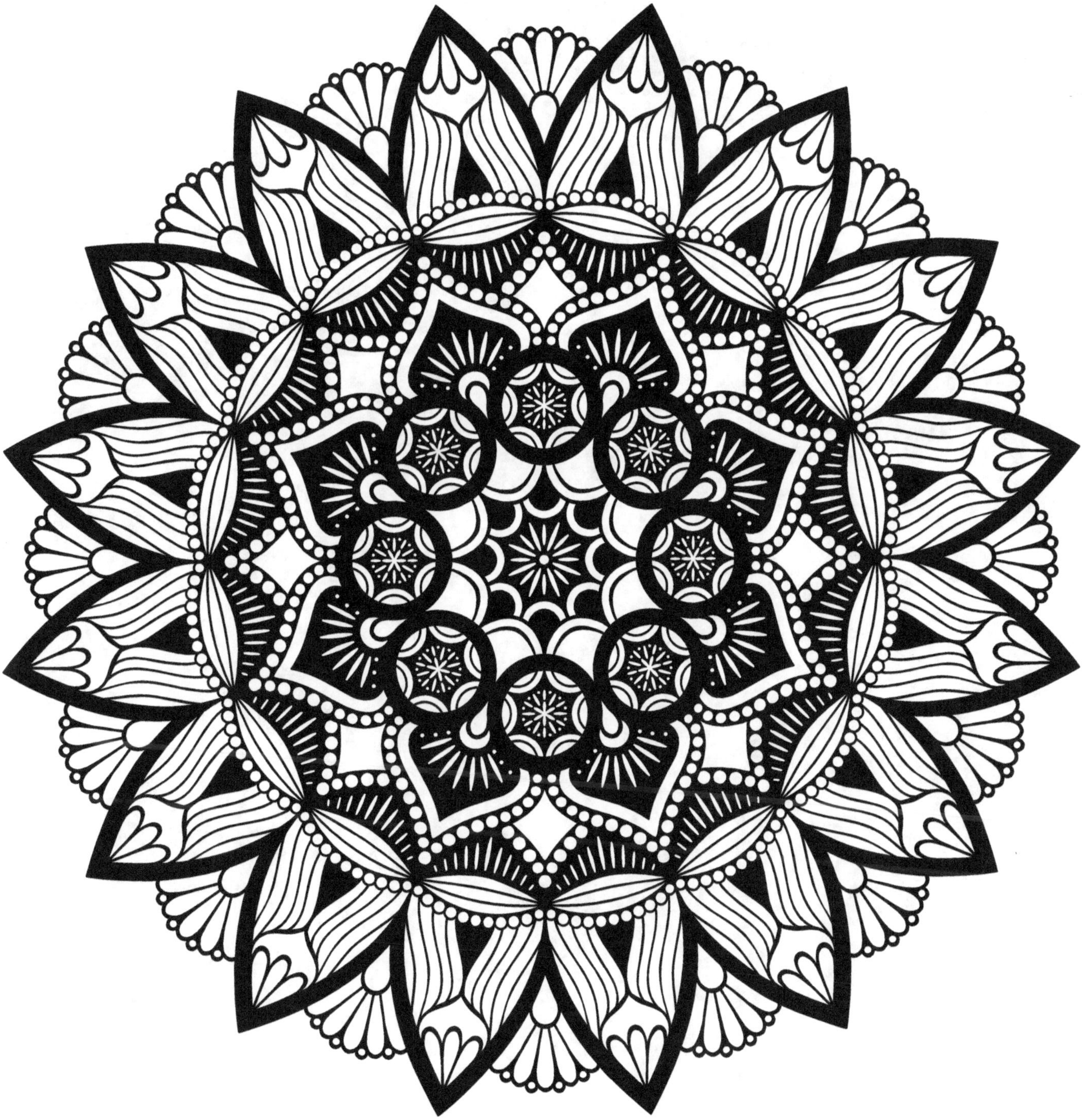

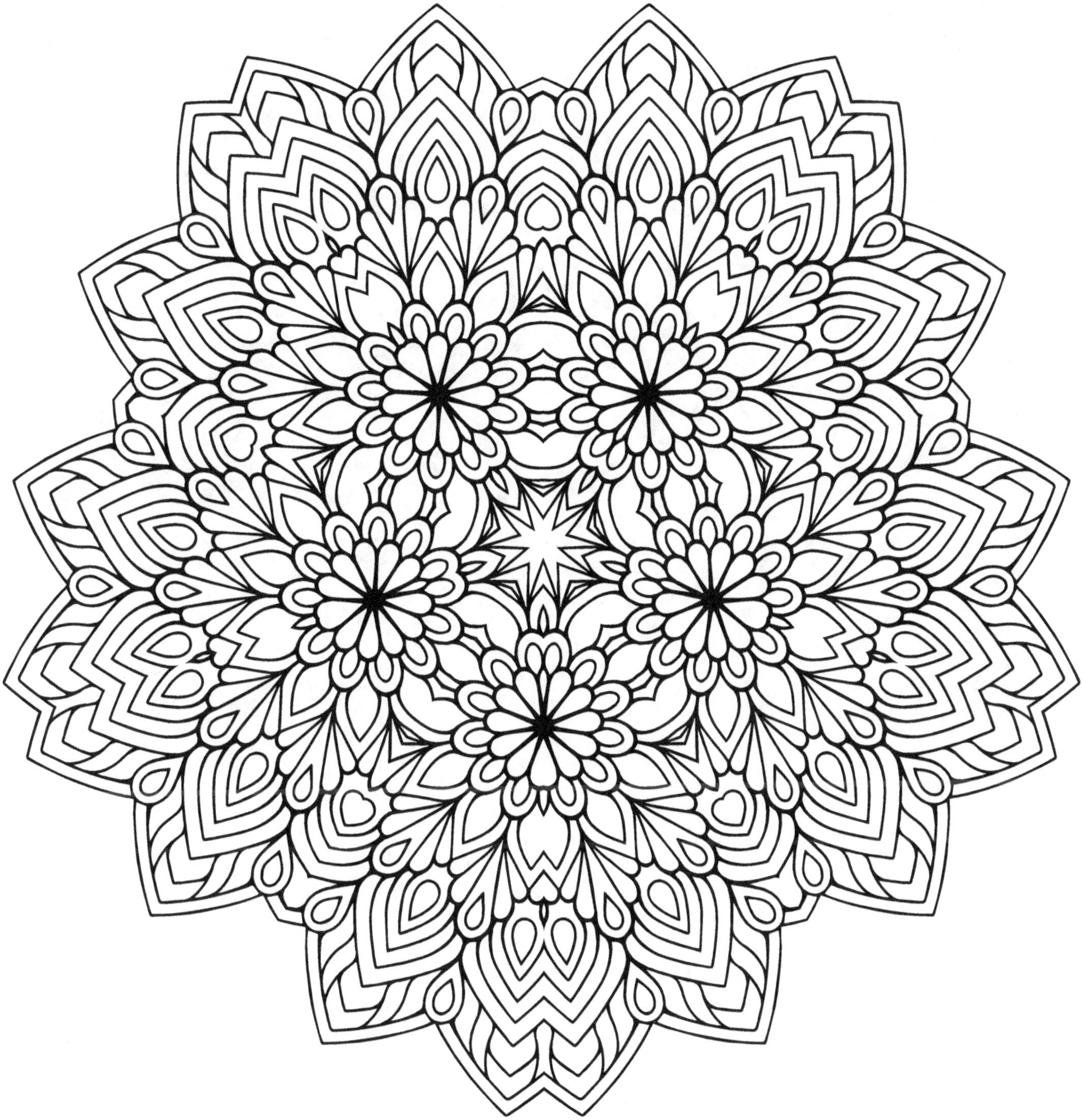

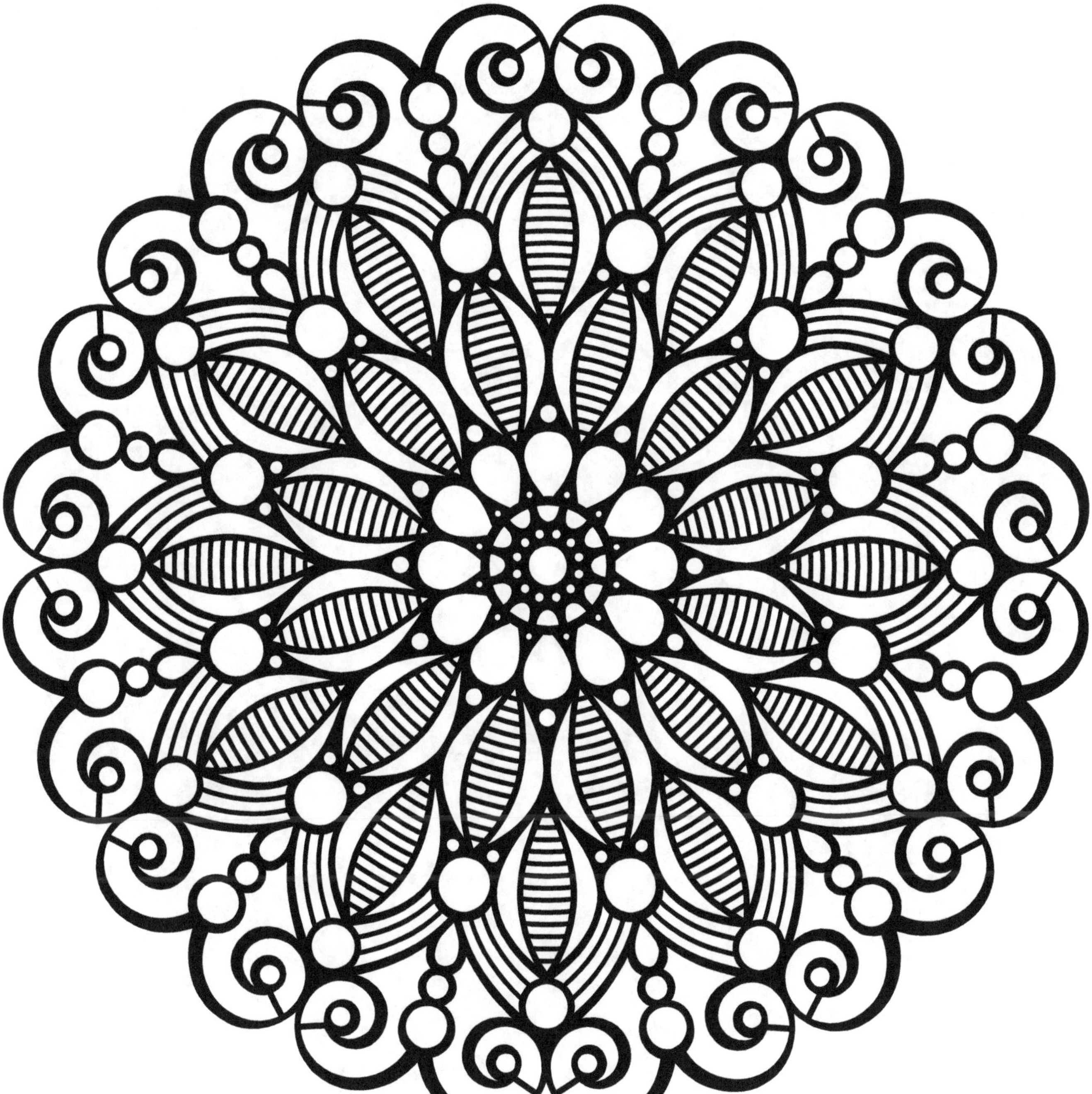

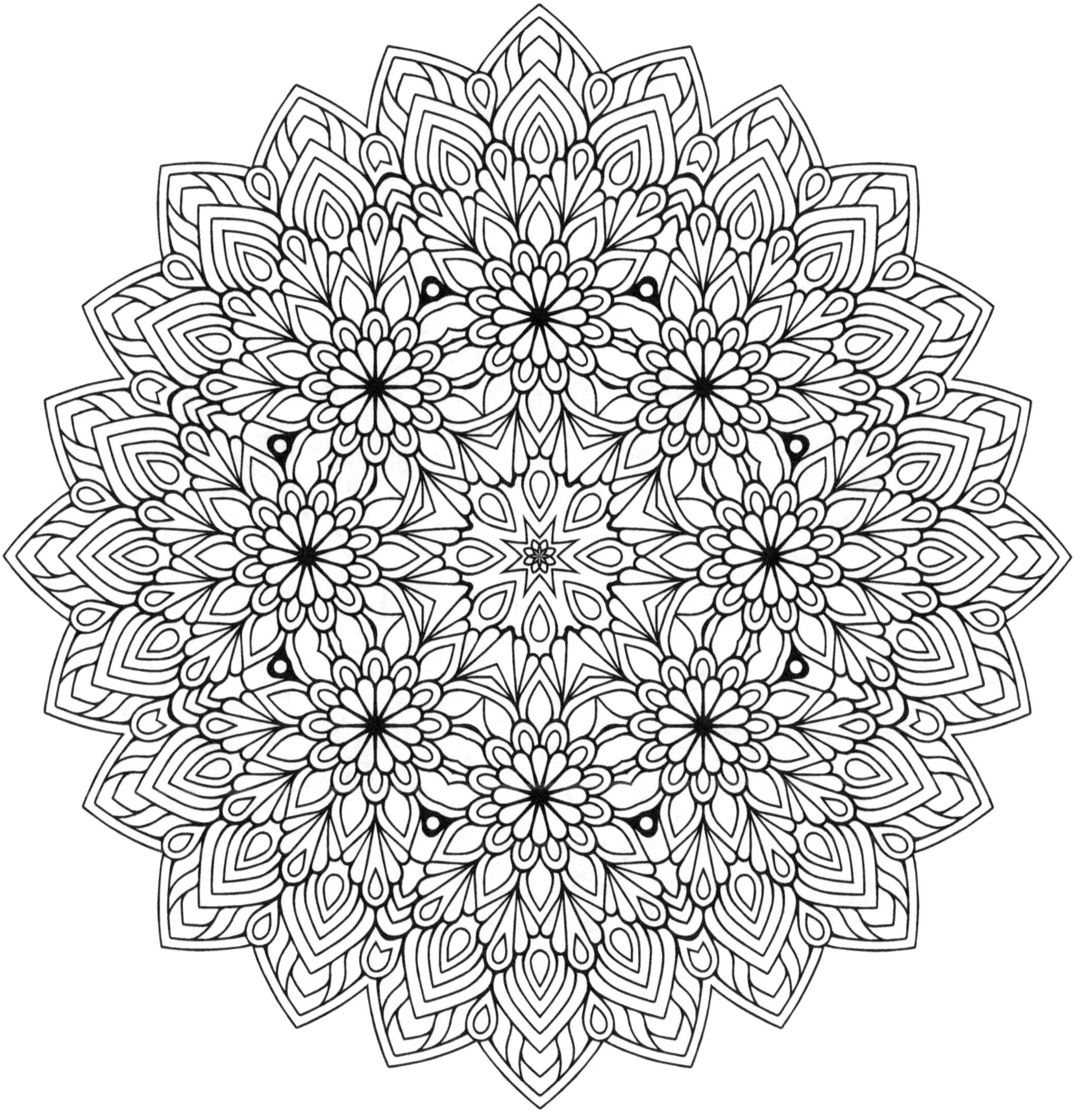

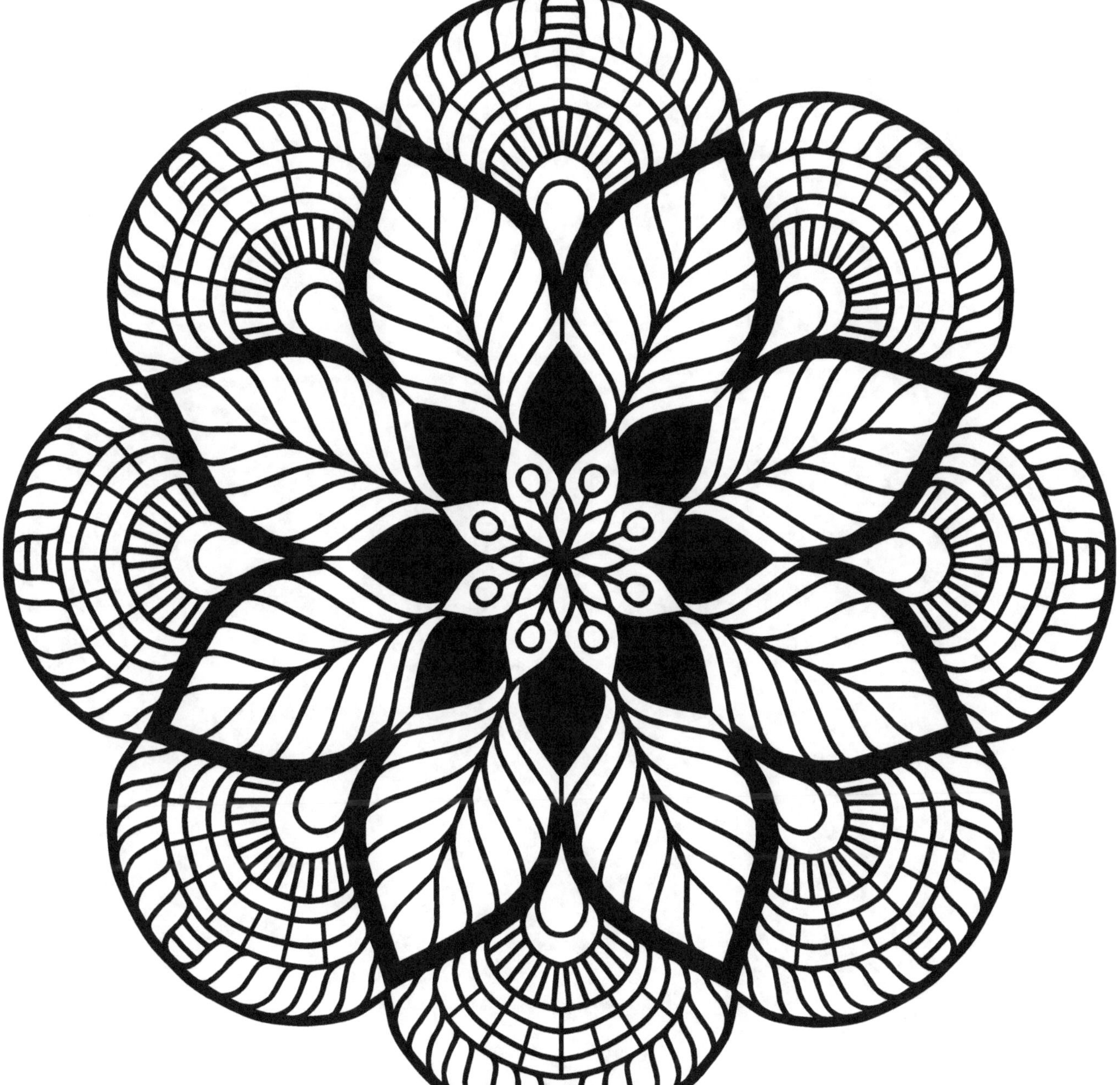

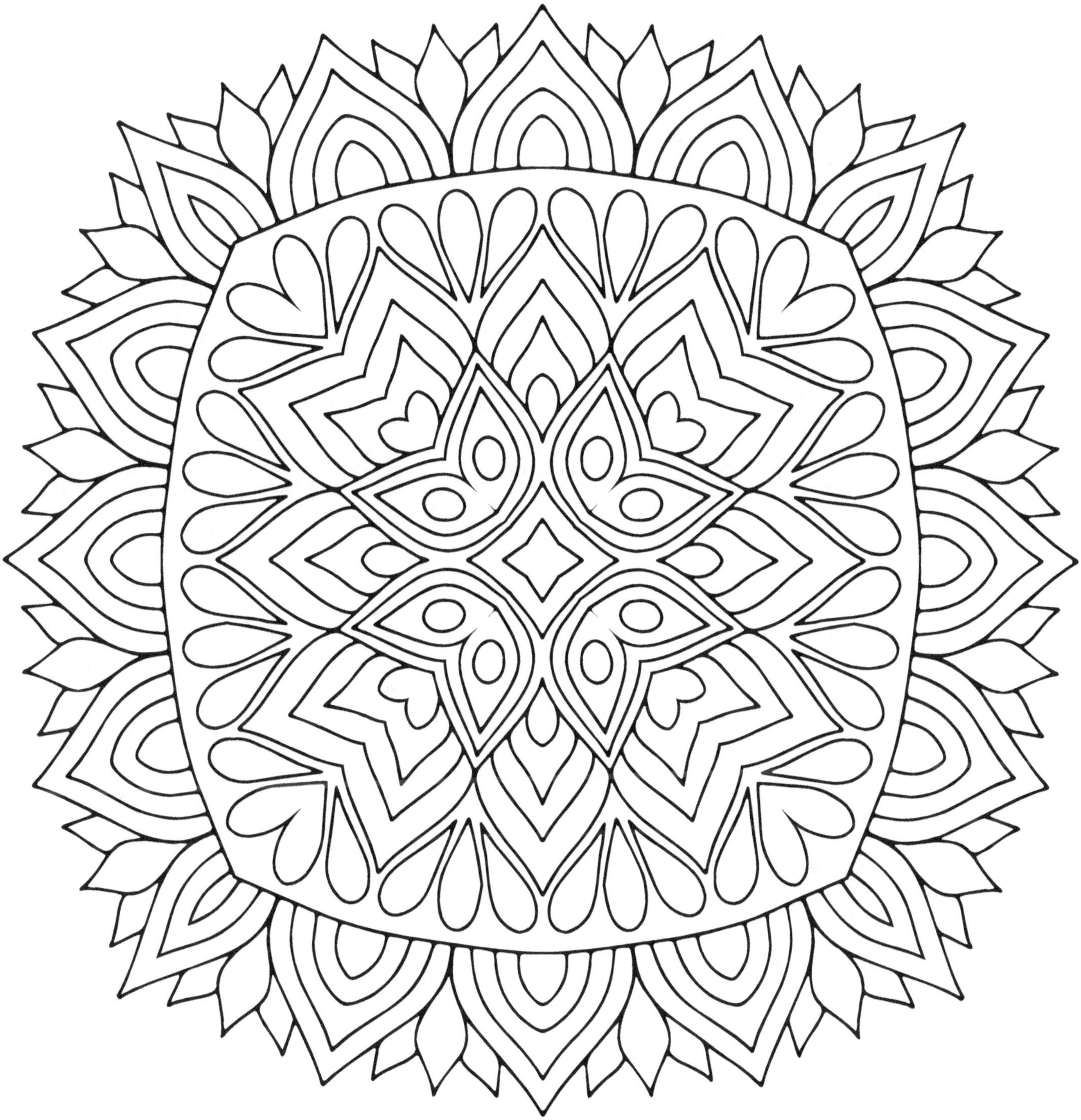

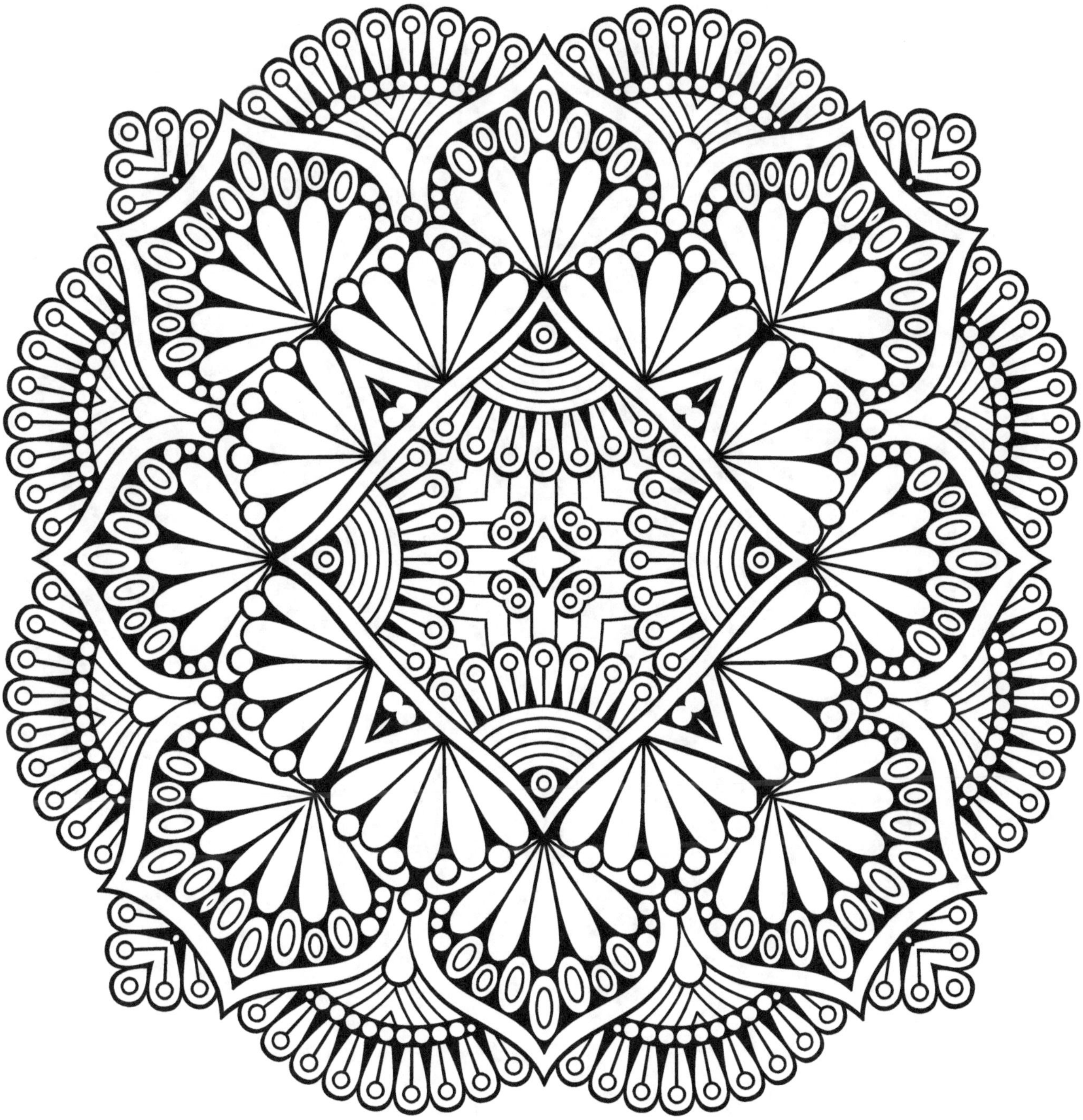

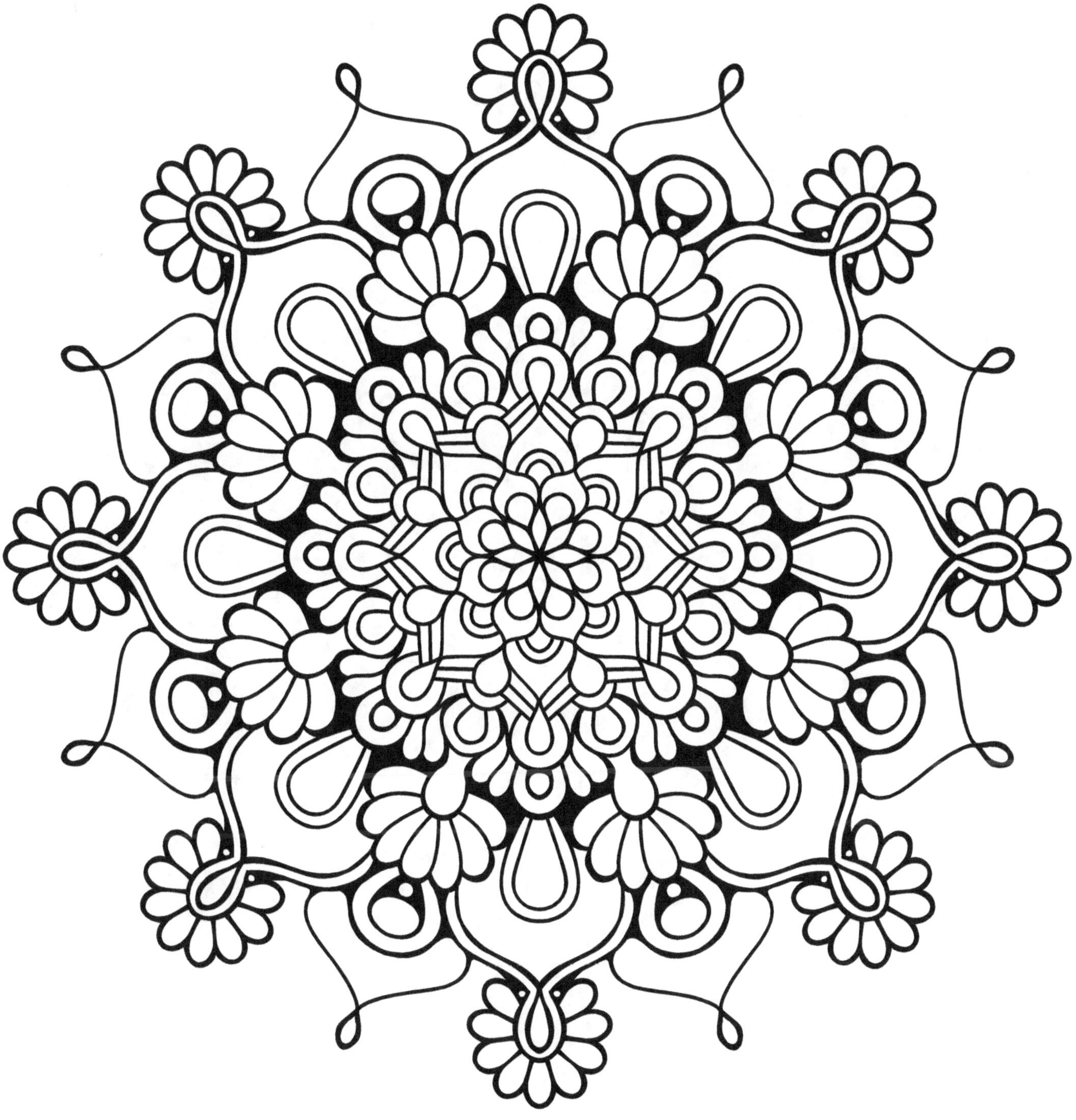

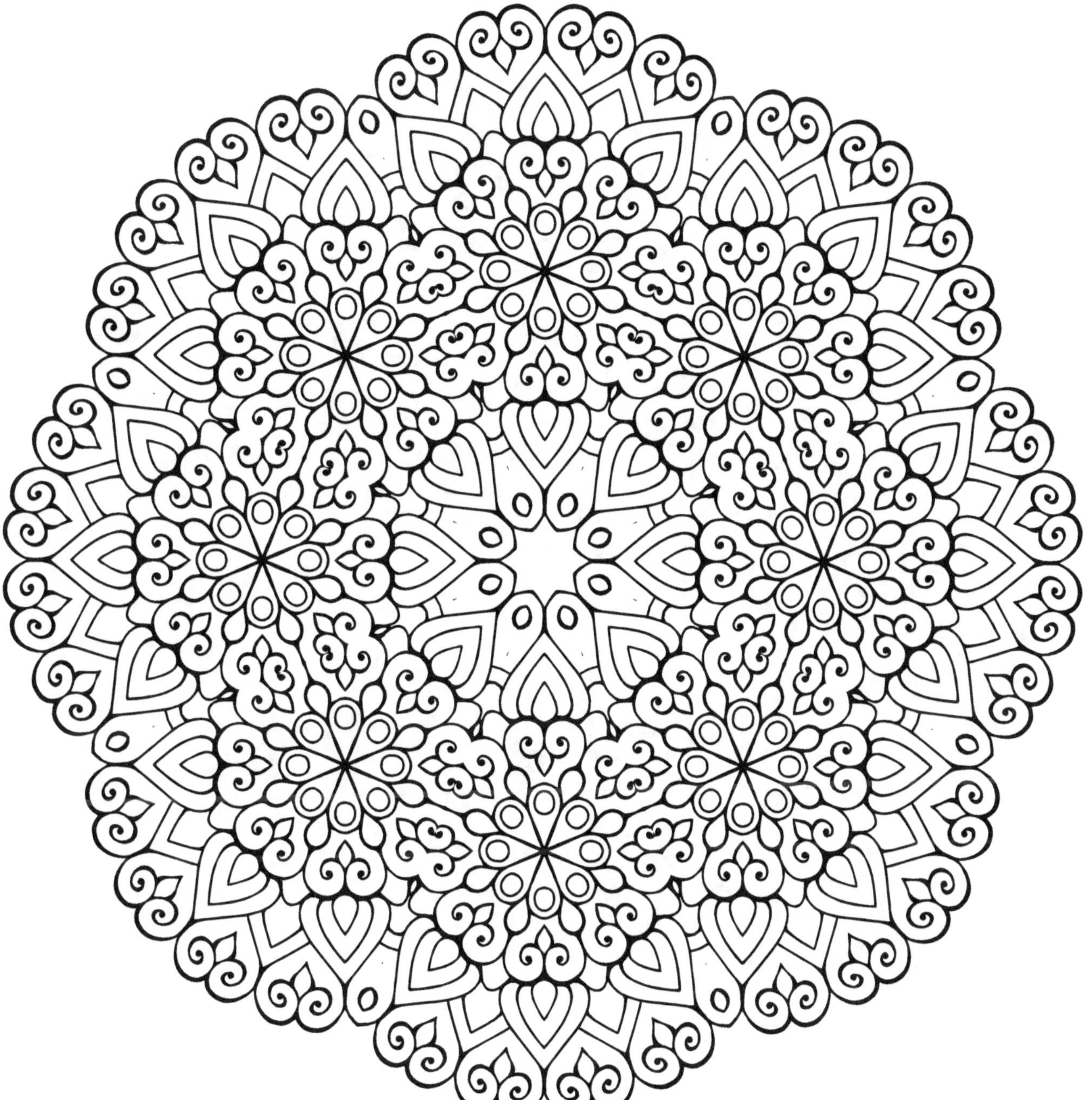

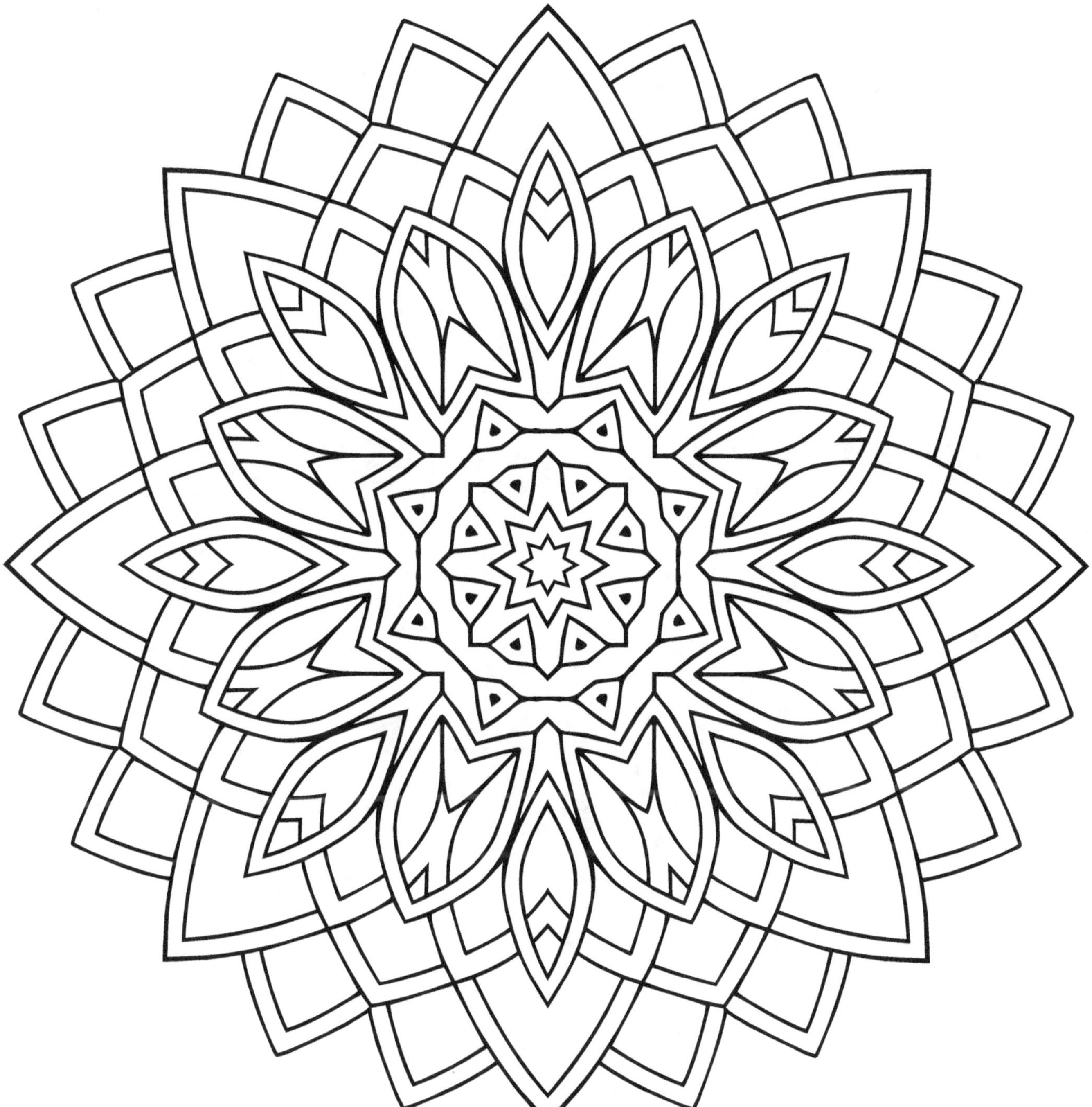

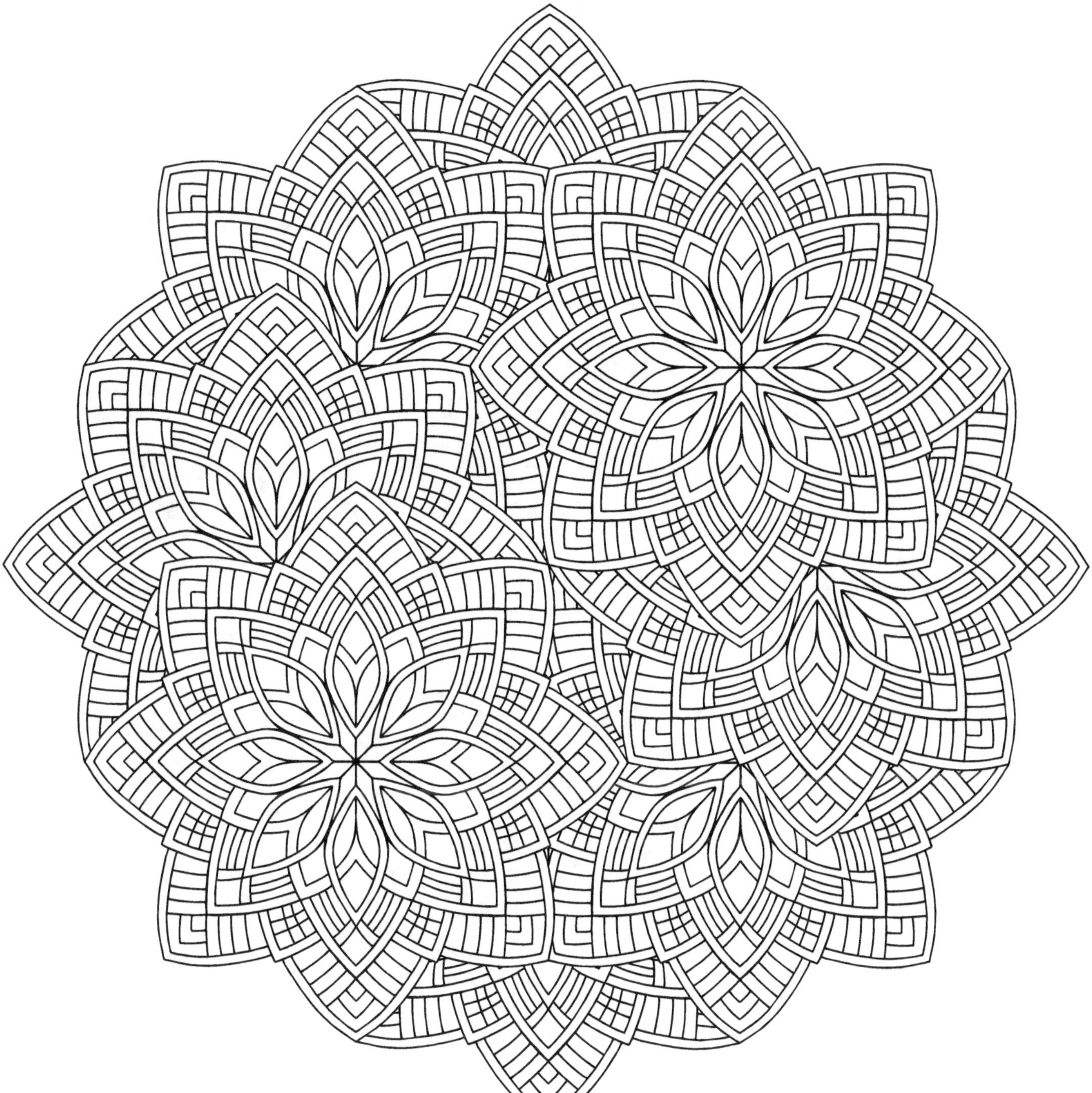

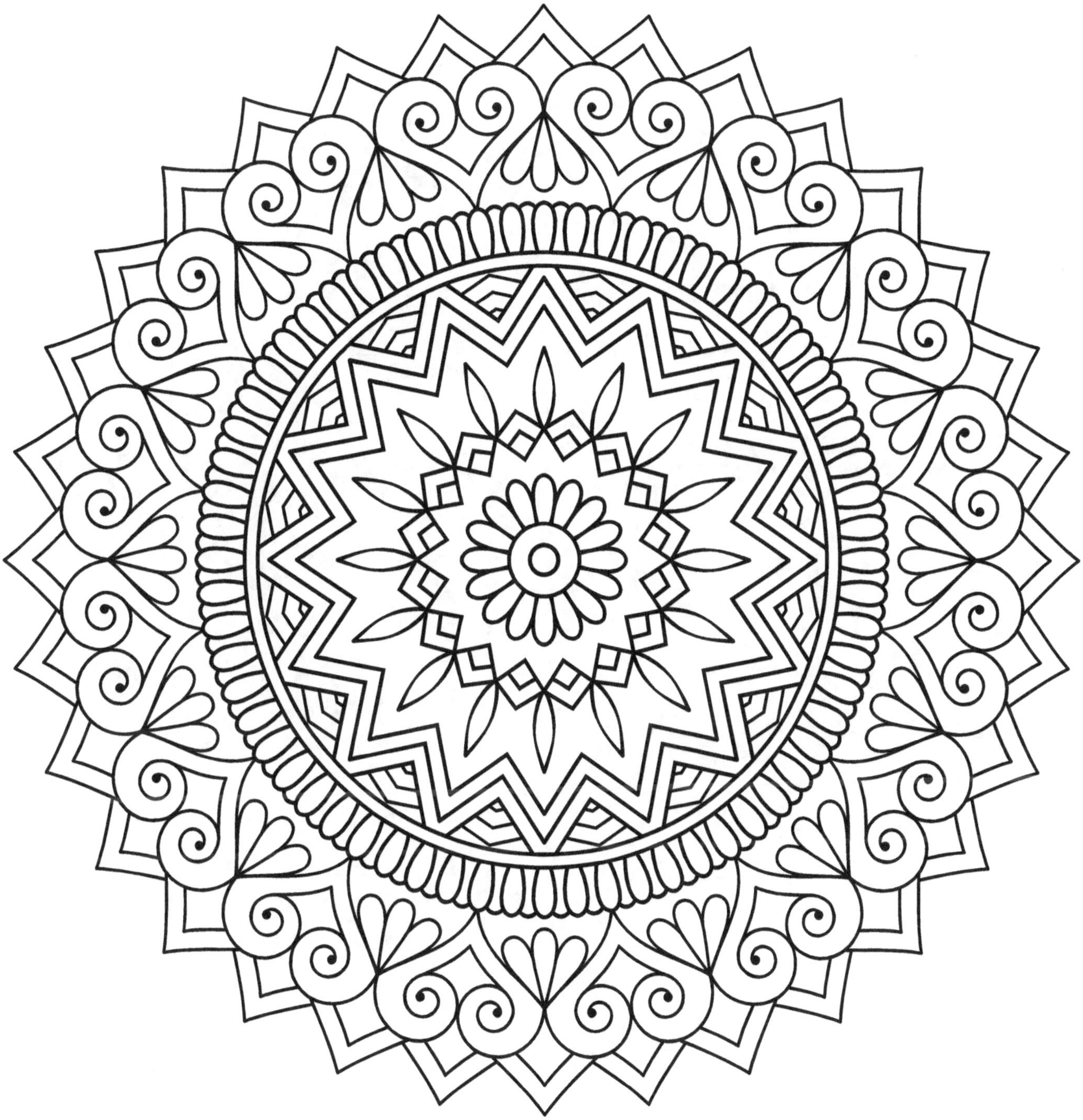

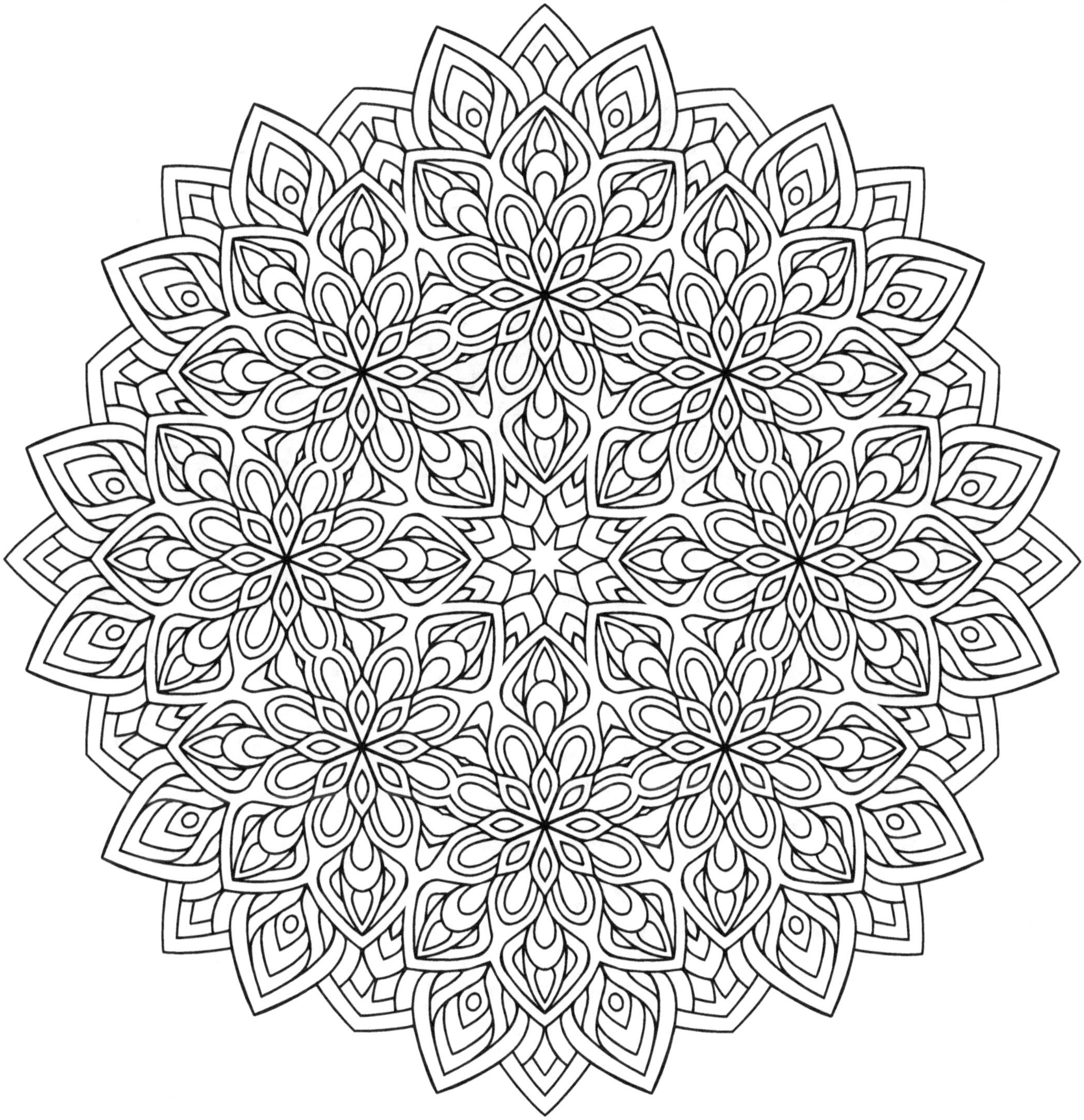

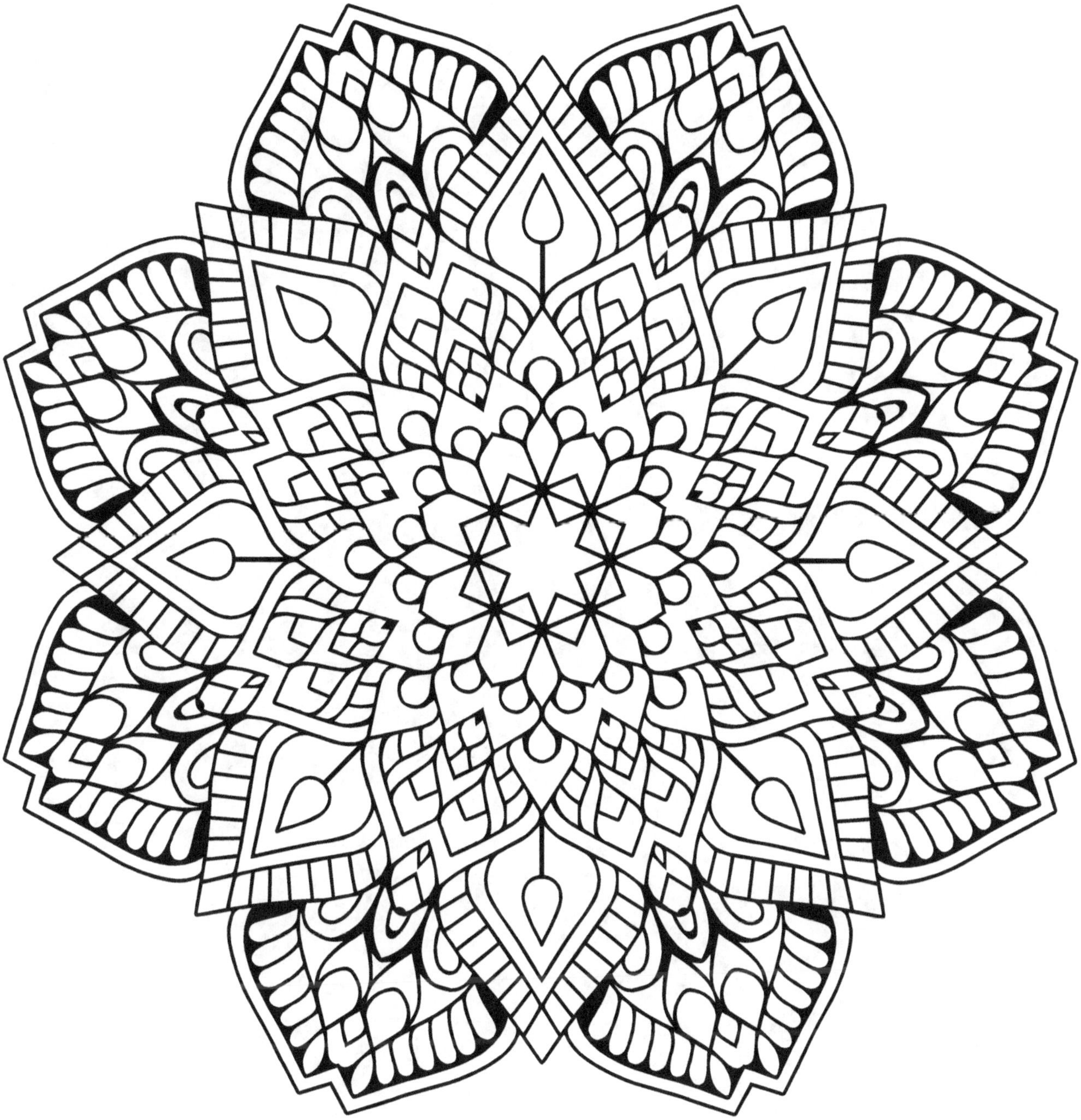

THIS BOOK BELONG TO

____

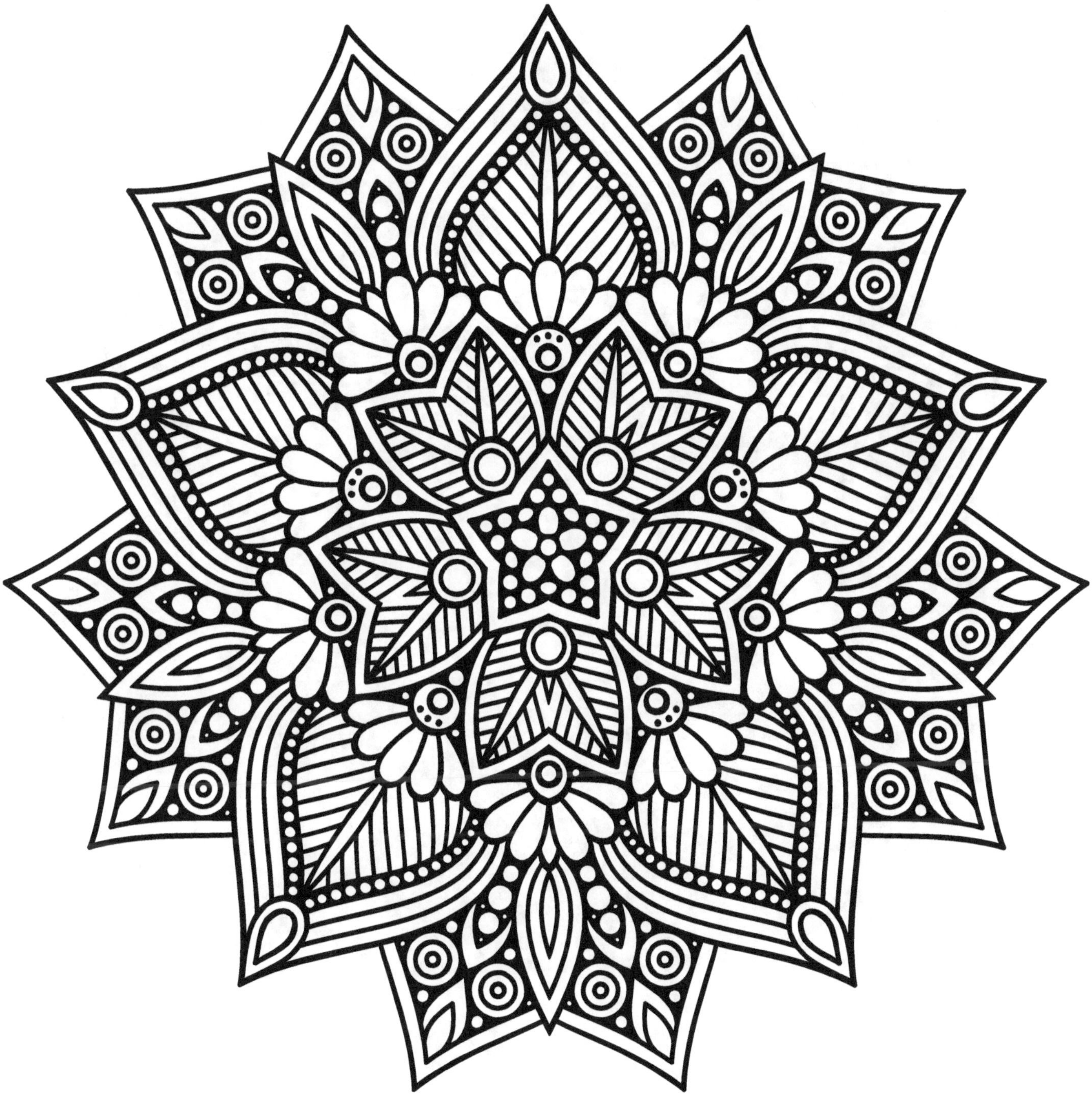

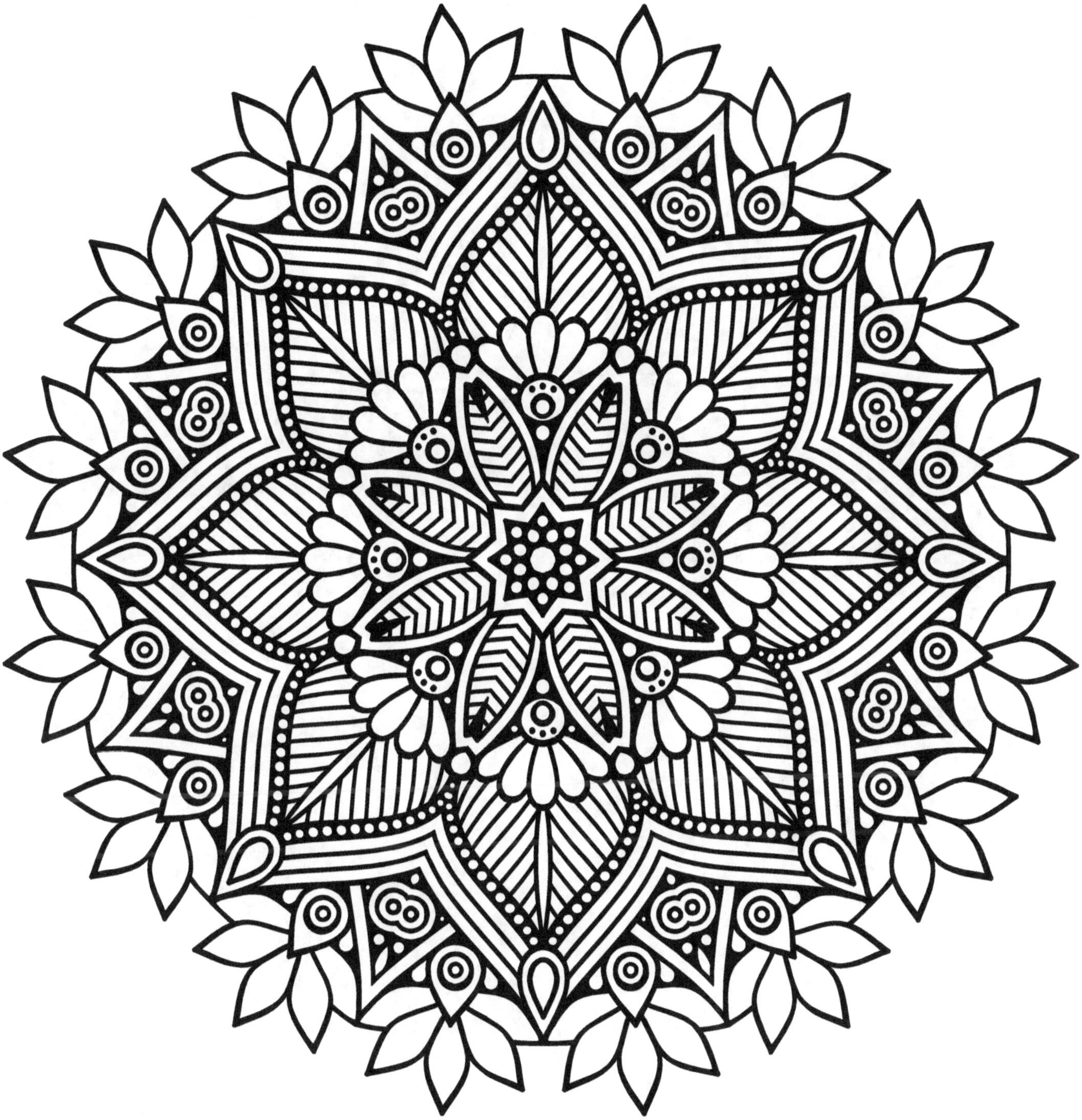

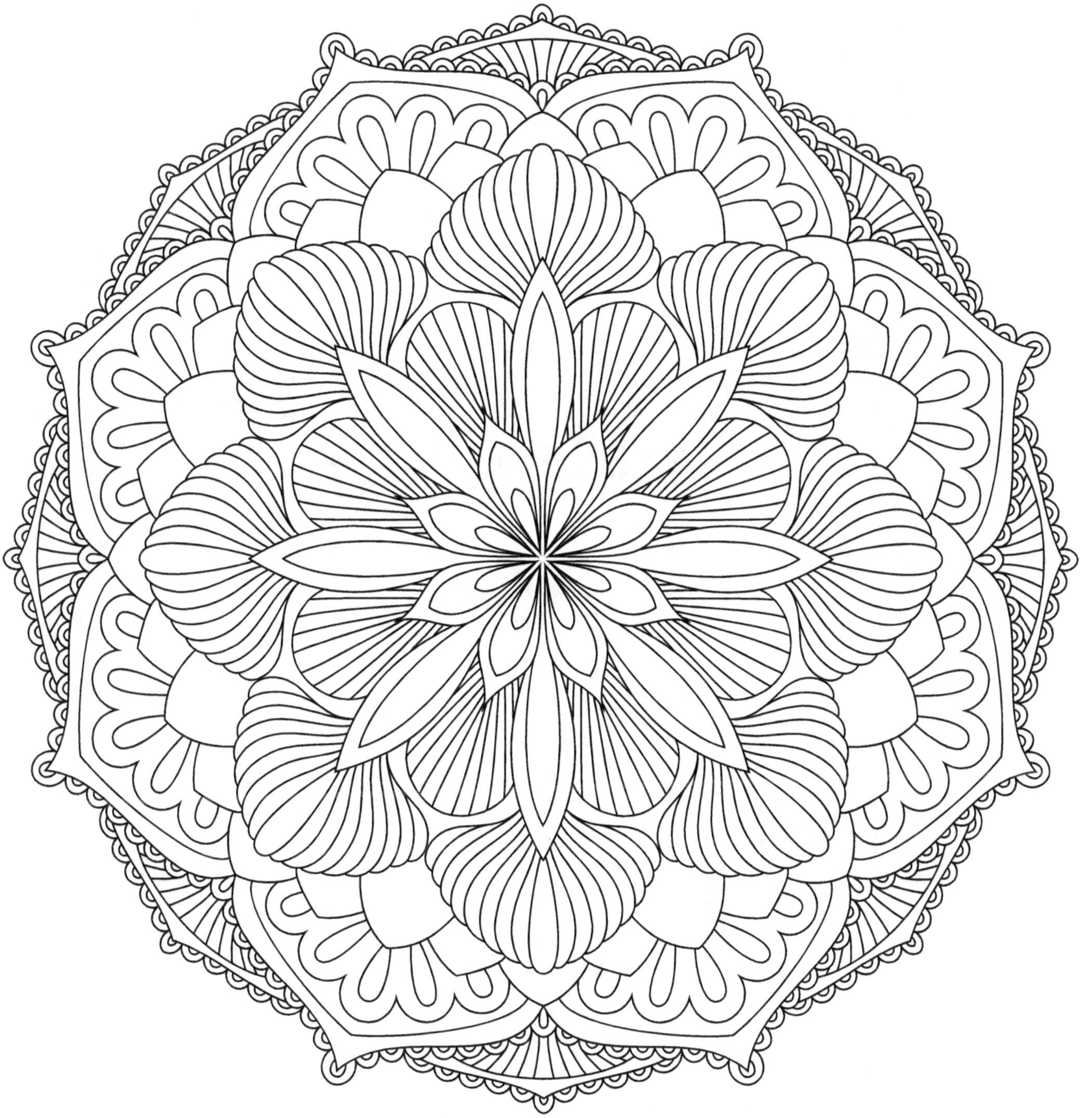

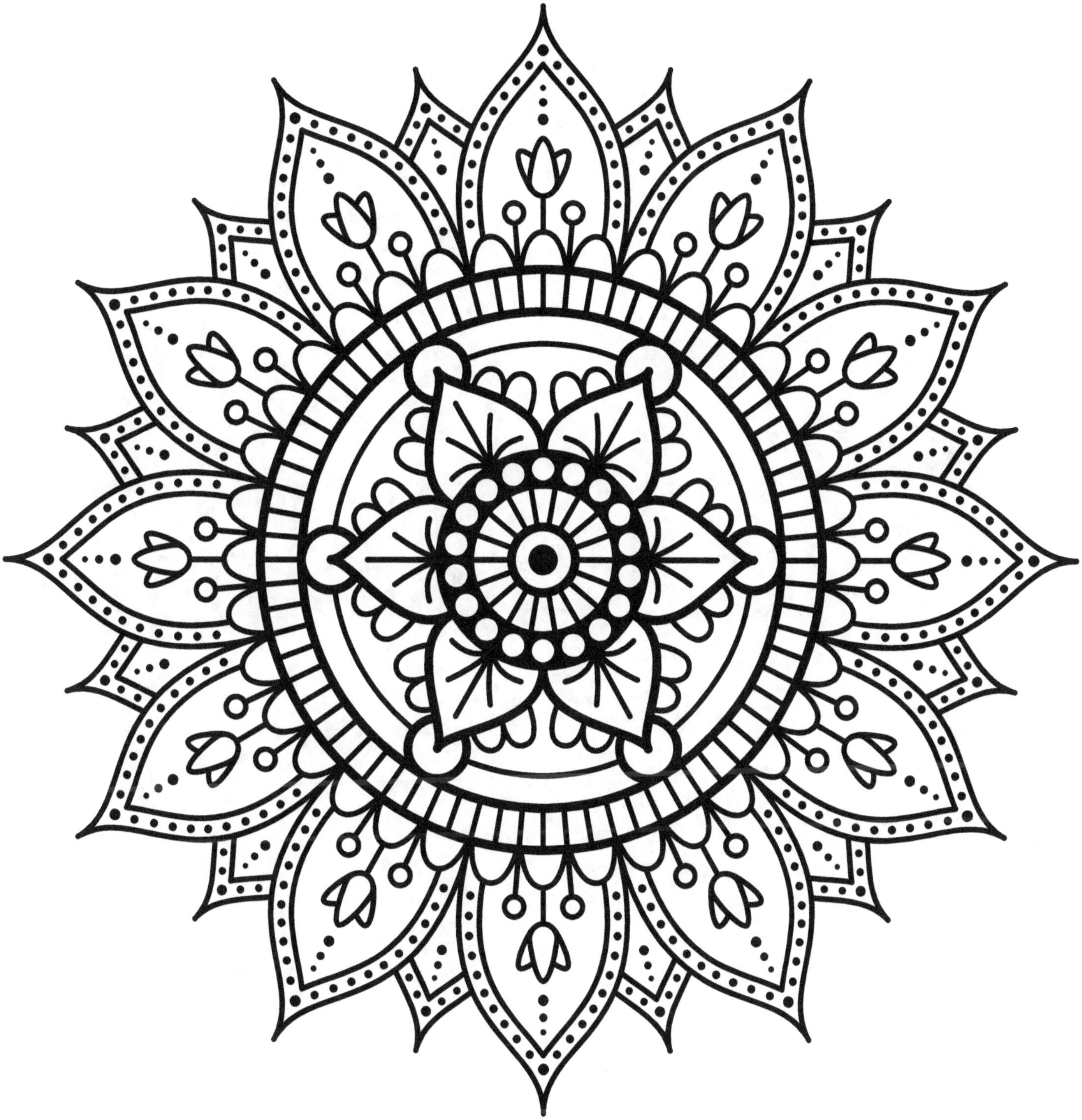

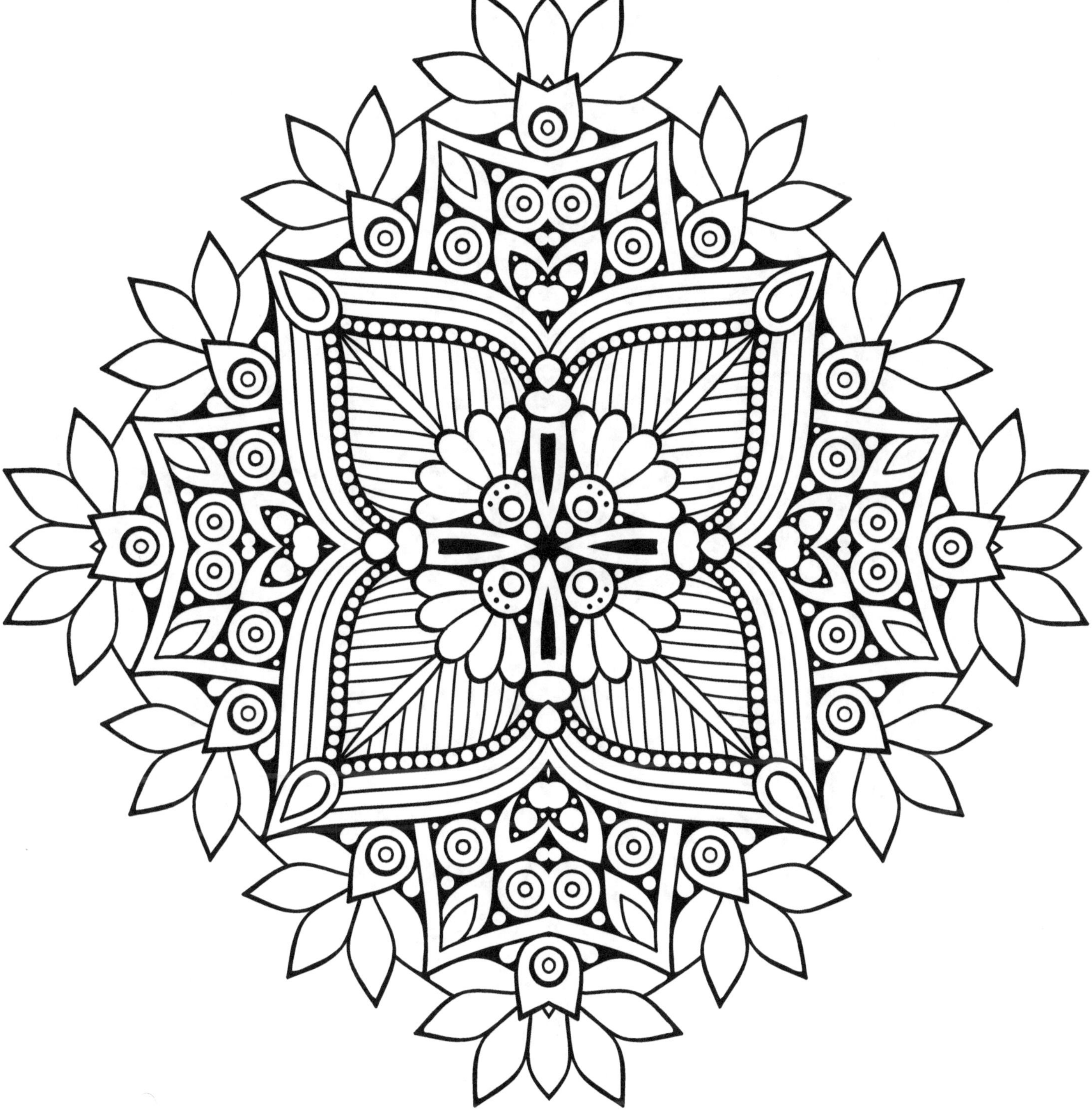

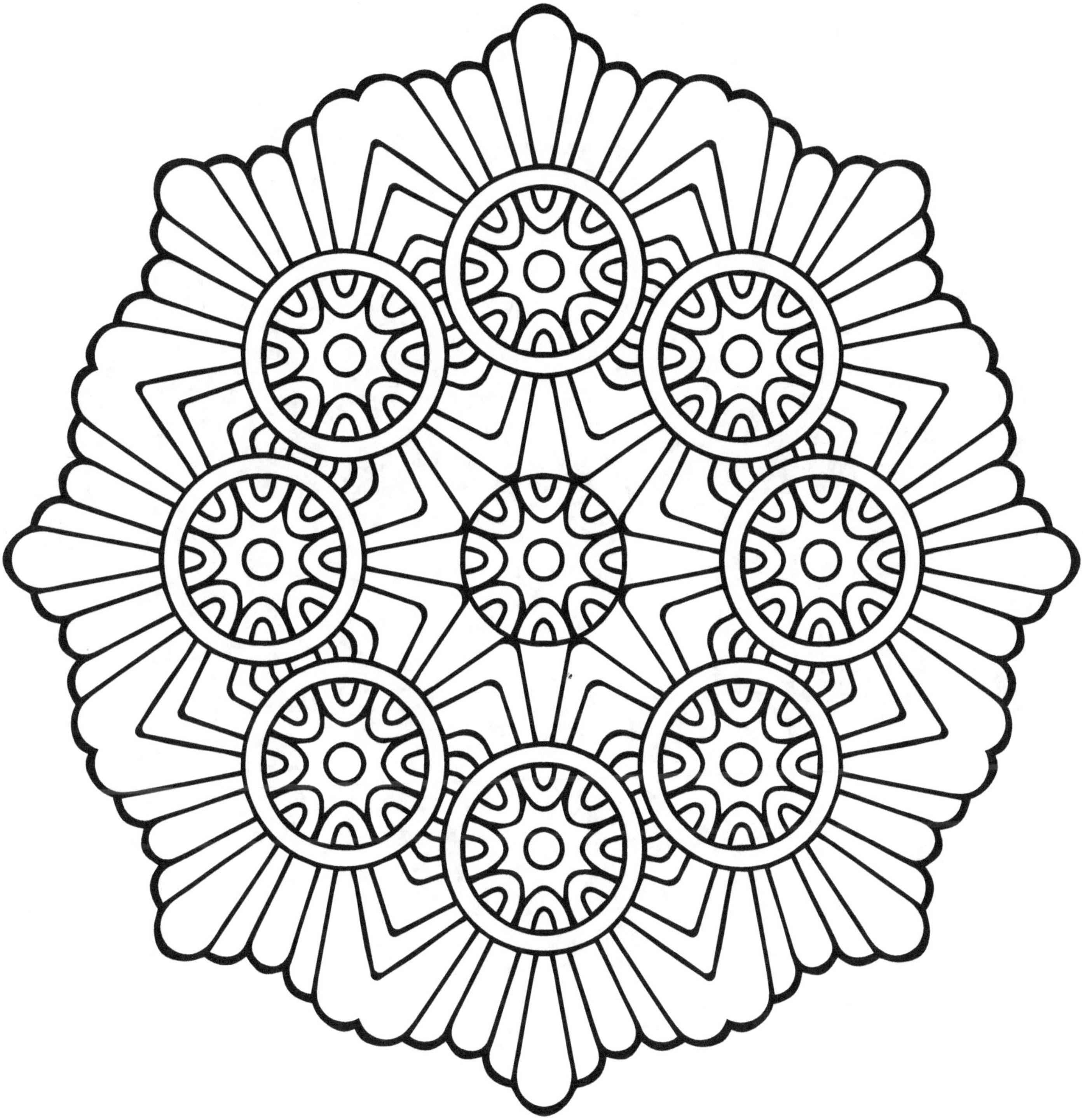

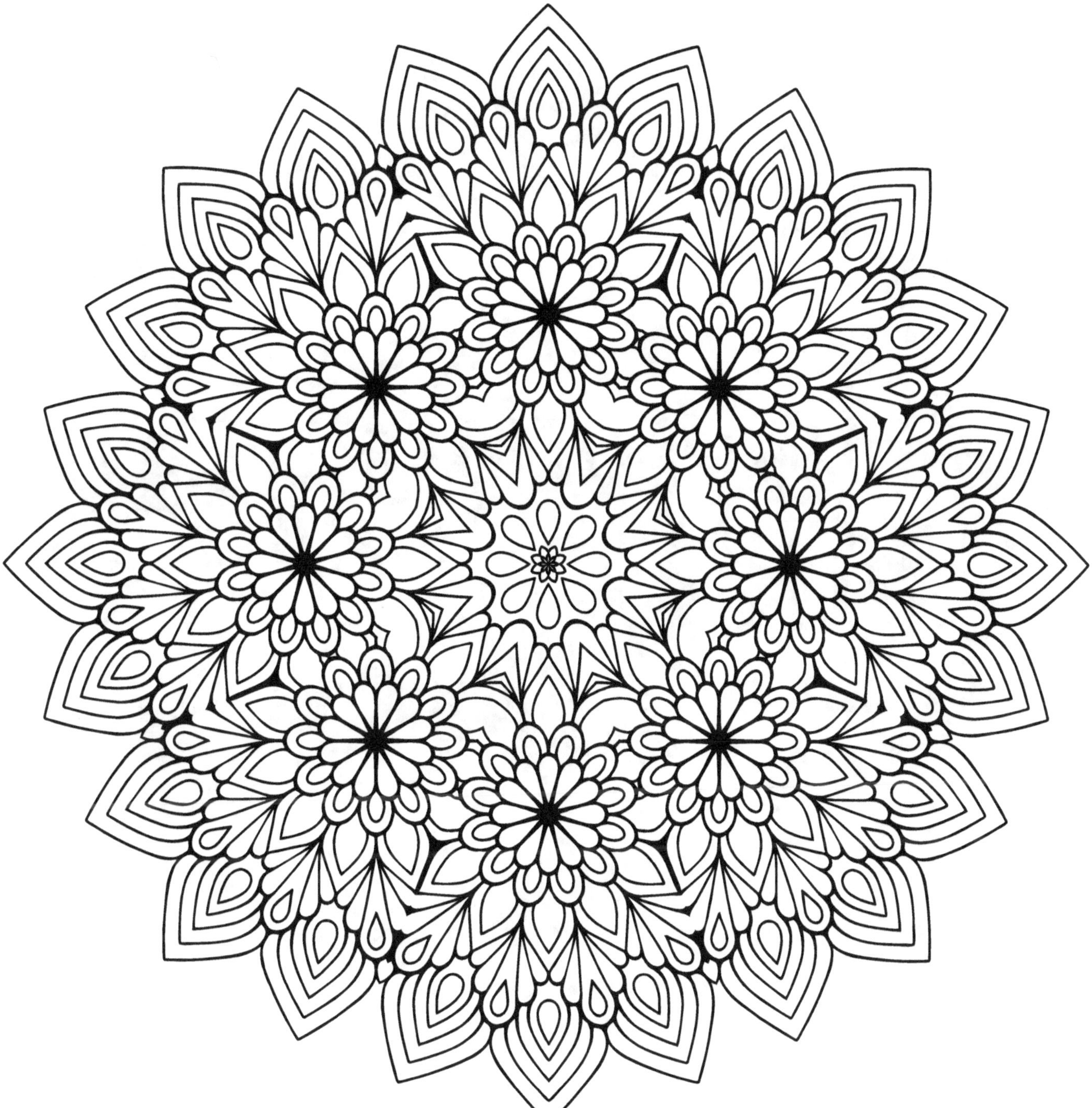

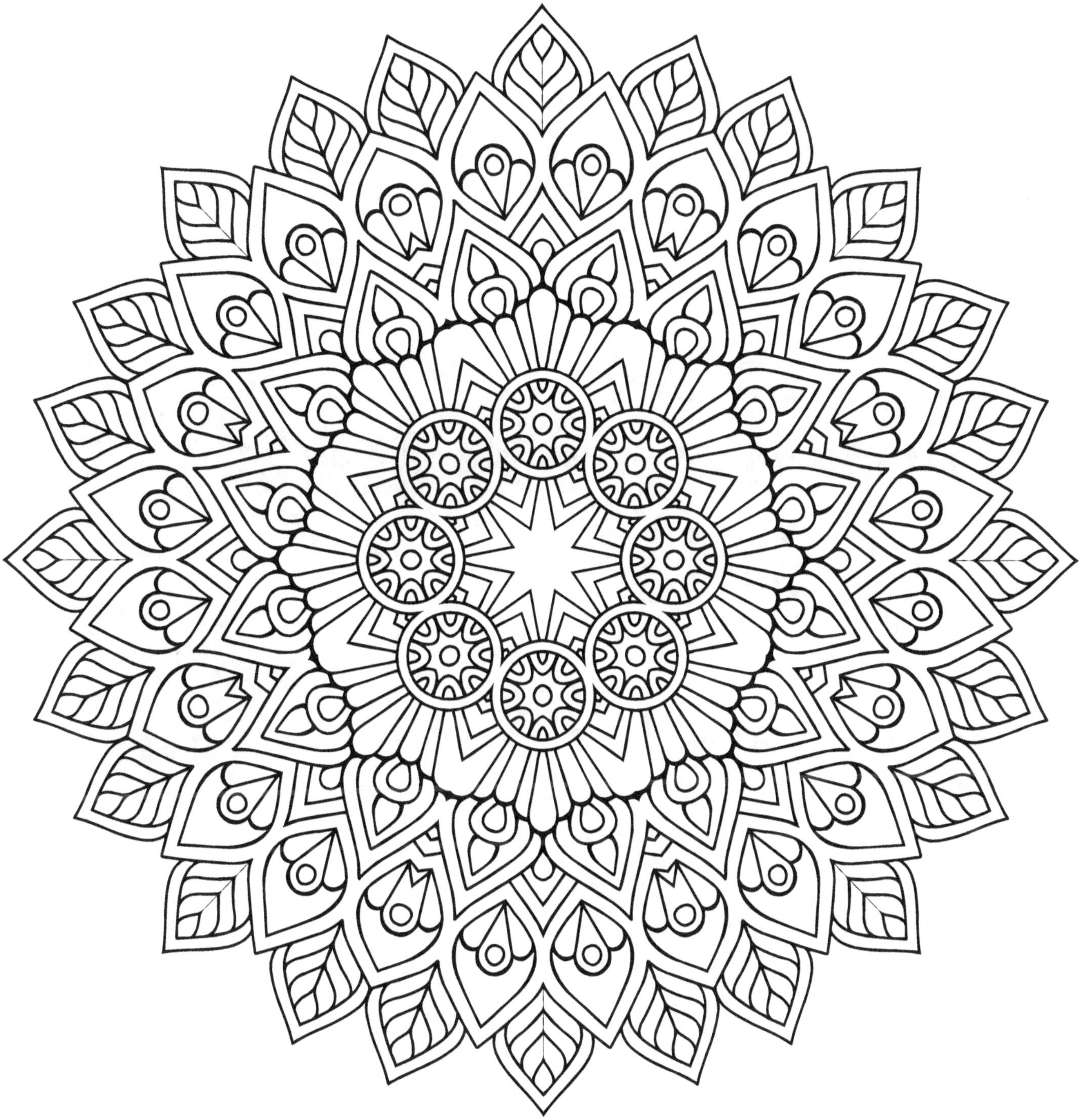

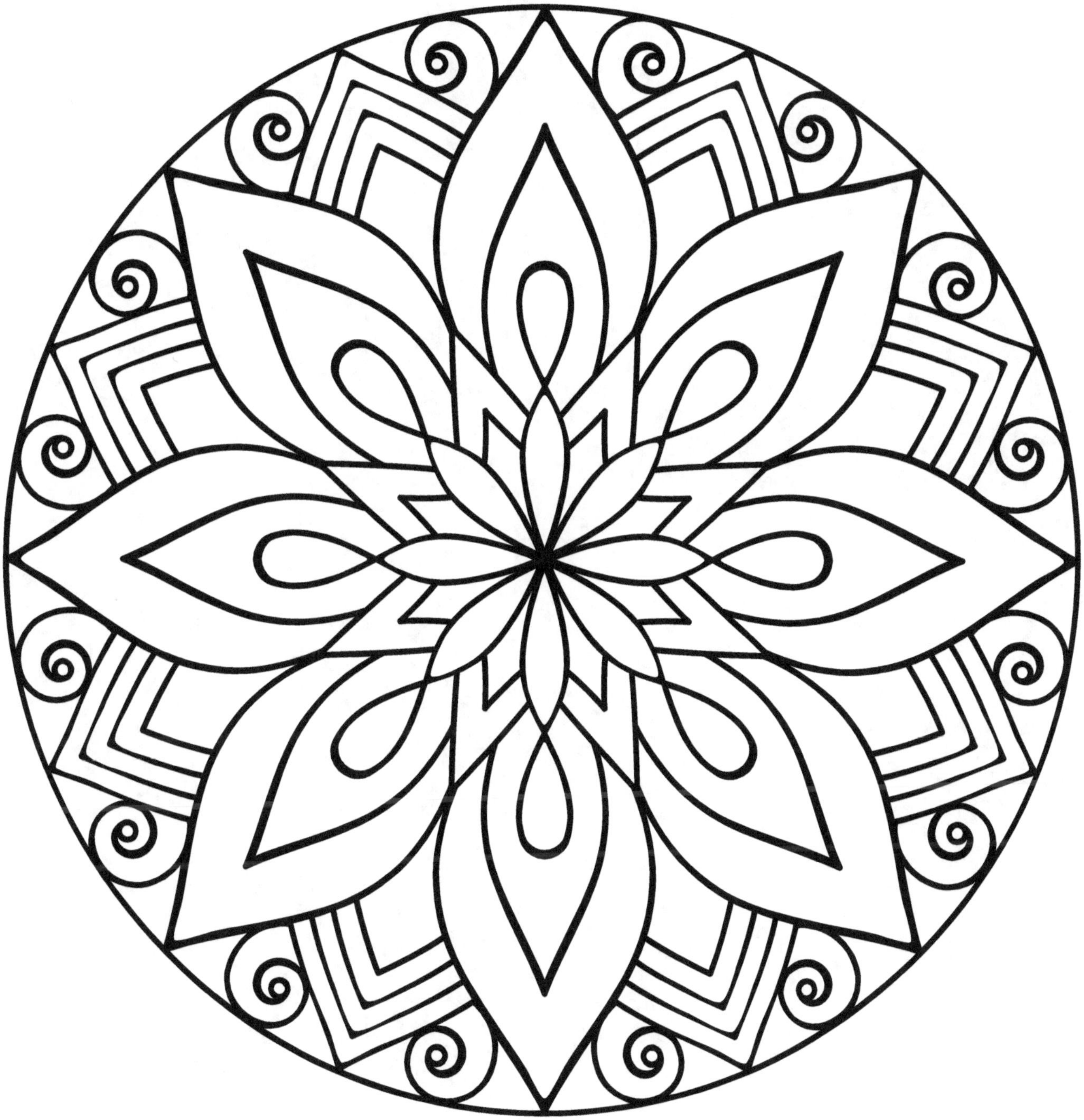

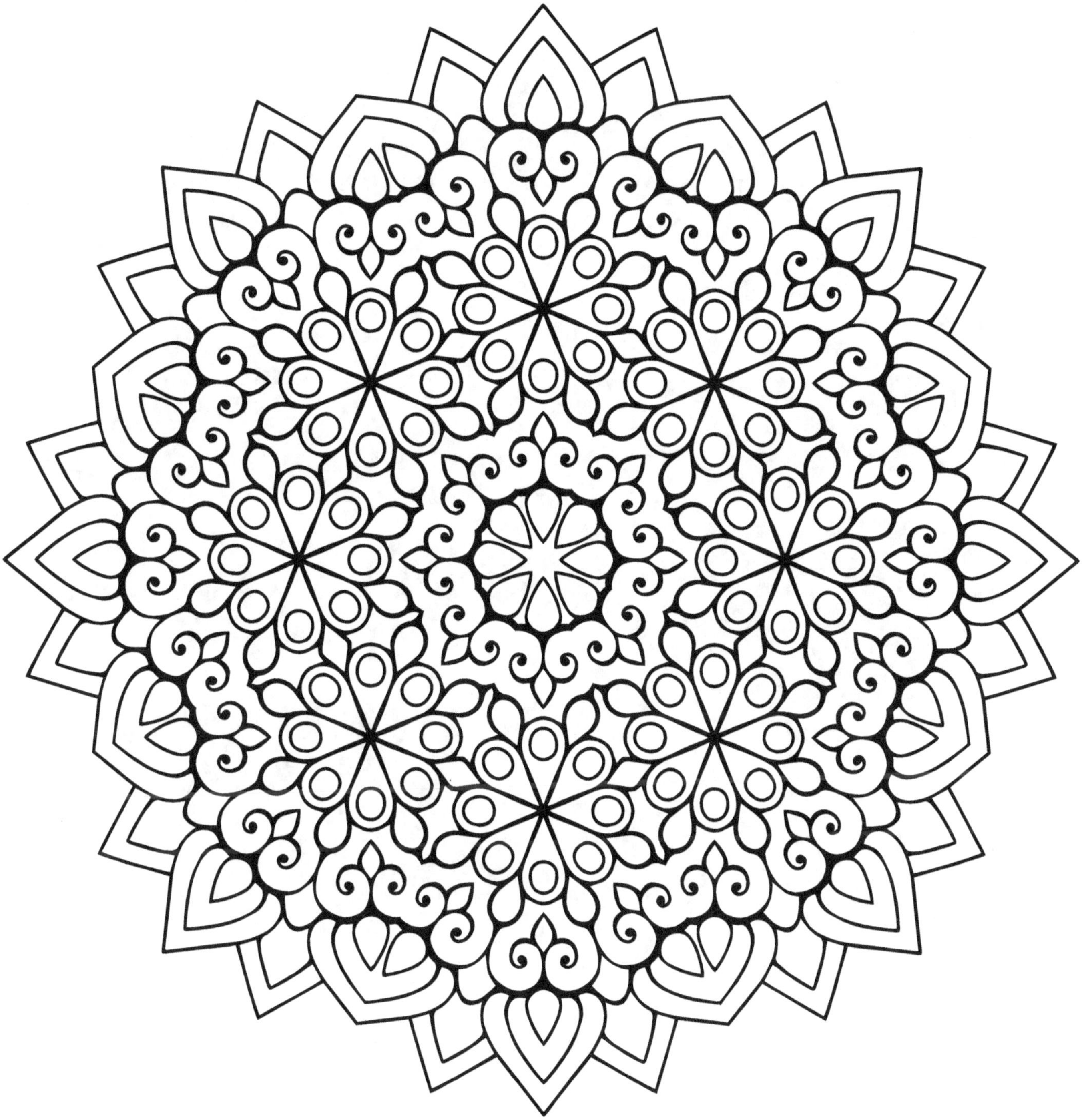

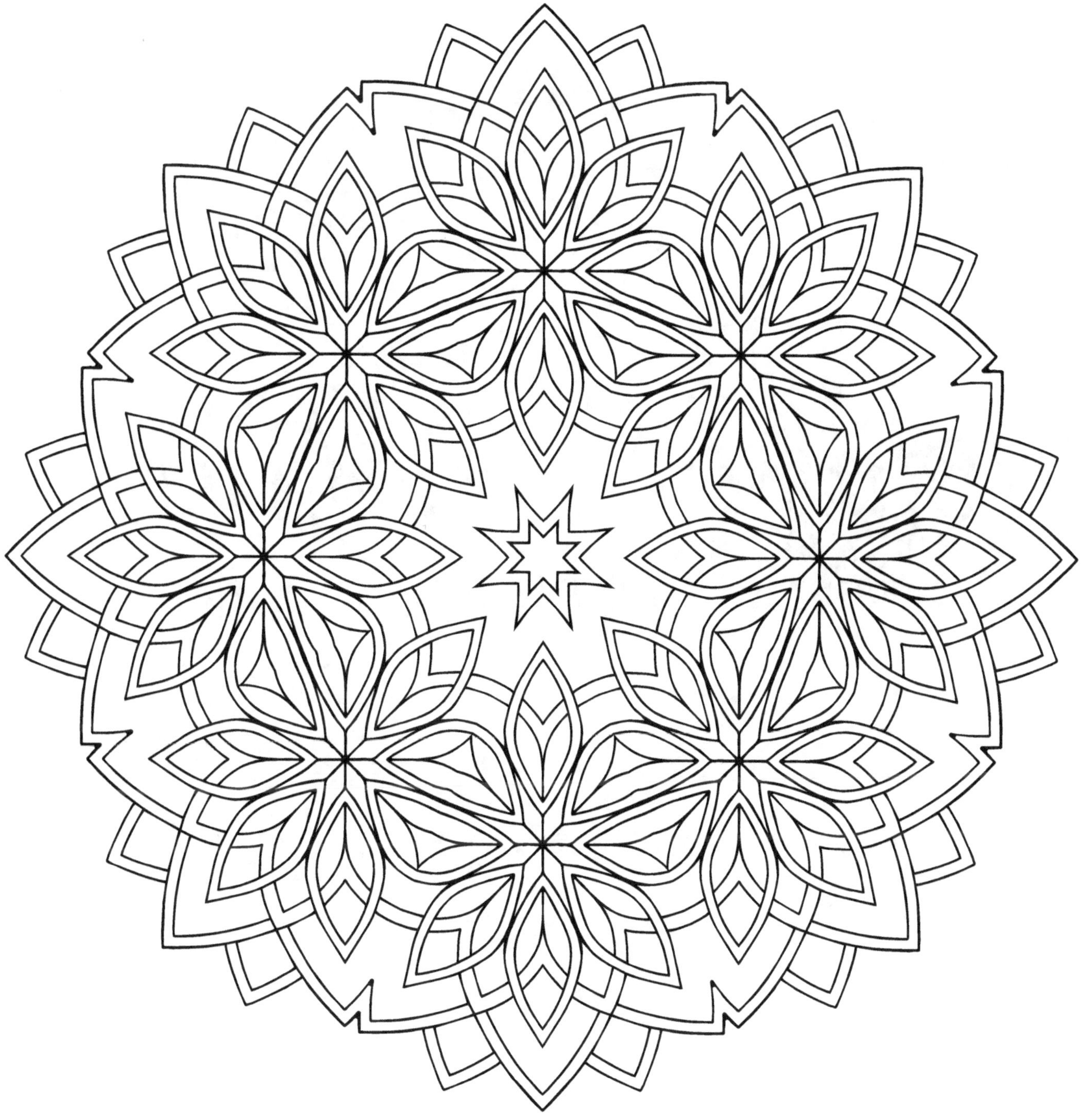

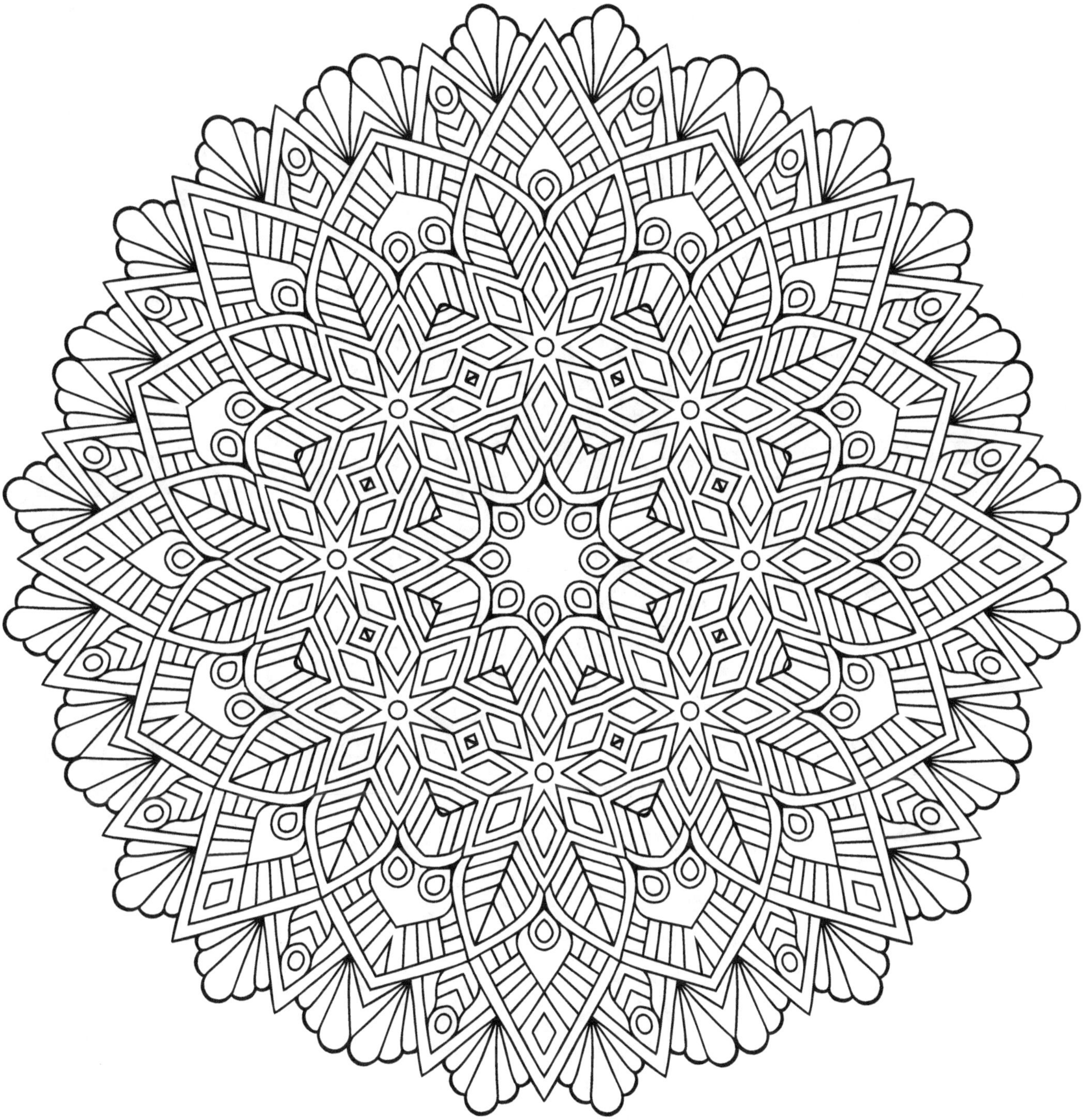

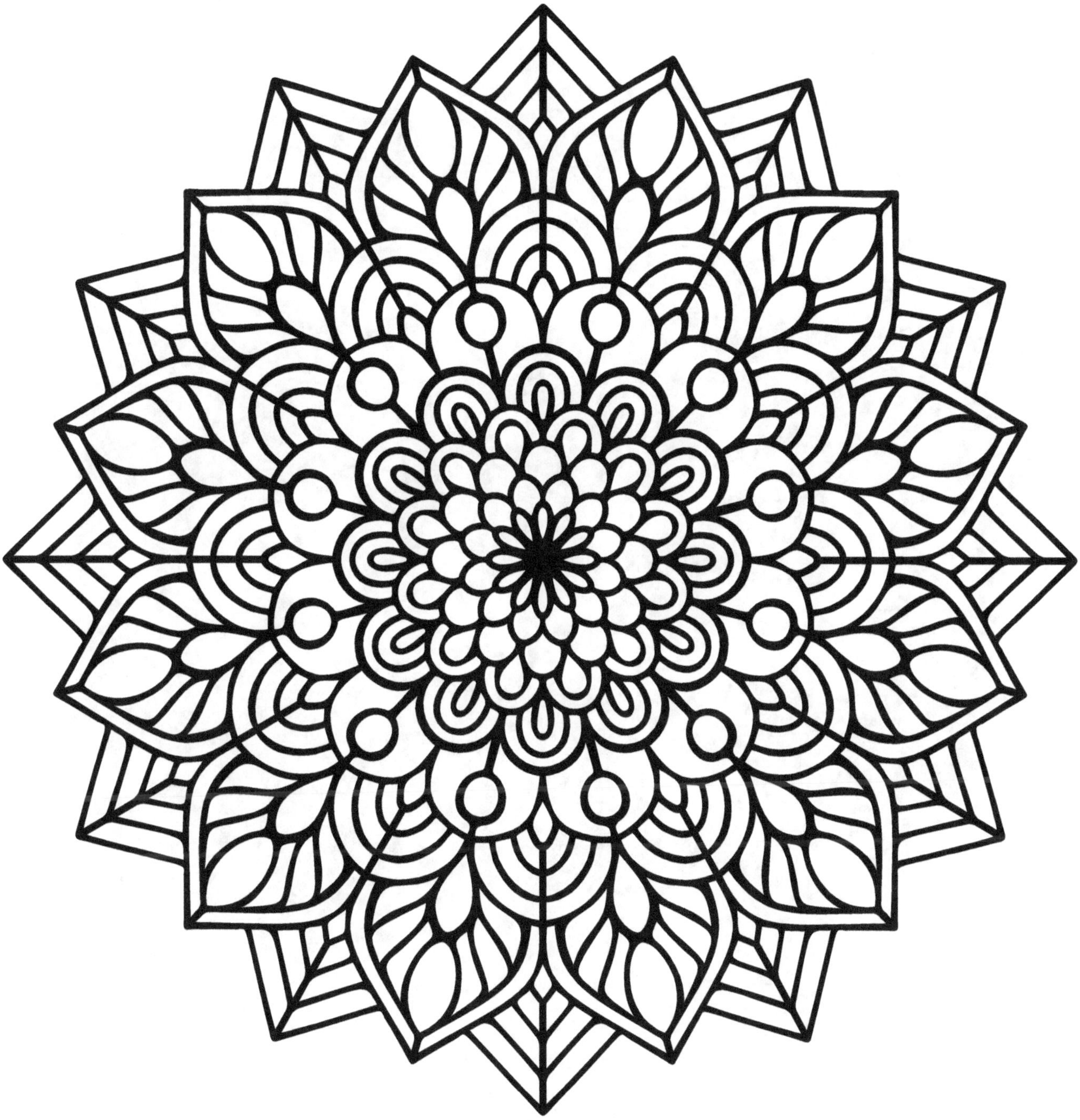

www.ingramcontent.com/pod-product-compliance
Lightning Source LLC
Chambersburg PA
CBHW081018170526
45158CB00010B/3084
* 9 7 8 1 0 8 9 8 8 7 4 7 8 *